ATLANTIC CROSSING

Atlantic Crossing

Stuart Crainer

The right of Stuart Crainer to be identified as the author of this book
has been asserted in accordance with the Copyright, Designs and
Patents Act 1988.

First published in 2015 by

St Giles Poets
The Studio
Highfield Lane
Wargrave
Berkshire, RG10 8PZ

A CIP catalogue record for this book is available from the British
Library

ISBN 978–0–9934017–0–1

Cover photo © Steve Litson

Printed in Britain by 4edge Limited, Essex

For Ro

Contents

PART 1: SEA

Sea equals

Wandering Dream

She has seen the world,
a wandering dream,
slogging down to Montevideo
and back up the coast;
to Australia and then summers
in Europe, Porto to Almada,
Grenada and Gibraltar,
always without complaint.

A child was conceived on board
and then the dream became a home.
Now, hundreds of miles from land,
a storm petrel follows the dream,
in and out of the waves,
a glide and a flutter, and on.

Atlantic Crossing

The Atlantic of the imagination.
The azure and dark water of *Las Canarias*
slips effortlessly into gigantic darkness,
the black water of fathomless depth.
A shearwater threads through waves
many miles from land, no other life,
no shipping, planes or playful dolphins,
just us, navigation lights
and expanses of sky slipping into sea,
not even a line between the two.

So, it begins: the water a broiling bitumen
black living pool crushed beneath
another simmering swell and another,
waves like careering horses
and the whole time the tides
and the currents a frenzy.
This is the ocean, thousands of miles of it,
laid in front of us; lonely vast despair
and the ultimate aquamarine heaven
devilishly combined. We rise, then fall;
the swell sweeps behind us and we move up
in some glorious ascension,

the water an inch or two under the stern.
From there you can see our watery world,
vistas north, south, east and west,
all endlessly deep and pitted with white tops.
And then we glide down in a fulsome fall.
Back on the tipsy level we can see little,
a bobbing glimpse of the horizon.

No more, no less, this is our Atlantic world;
the beginnings of our journey.

First Night

Climbing the stairs from the cabin,
I wasn't ready for what was above.
At the top I looked out.
It was as though cymbals crashed.
The seas, swirling thick smoke,
rose above us when once they had been below.
Their sound was sibilant fury,
their menace heightened by shades of darkness.
There was no moon. There was no pause.
I stayed in my slippery seat,
hit full in the face by the sea.
This was some dreadful initiation,
a first night stricken with nerves,
a debut of disasters, a stumbling entrance,
a presage of things to come, a song title:
"First night Atlantic blues."
I laughed and was promptly sick.

We Sleep

We sleep on a moonless night.
The dark is intense. Now, here.
Somewhere there is light,
breathtakingly brilliant perhaps,
but not here in the ocean's midst.

We sleep on a moonless night.
Still the boat's roll moves us
and its fraught, noisy breaths
catch on the air, threatening
to wake us, to shake sleep to life.

We sleep on a moonless night.
The boat strives, a steady six knots,
and the wind at eighteen,
eating into the ocean's curve,
nibbling a slow way forward.

We sleep on a moonless night.
What else is happening? We care not.
Here is blackness and noisy peace,
the bridling ocean held at bay,
awaiting the tired first glimpse of another day.

Luminescence

1.

A glow worm on the stone stairs.
An August half-mooned night
and the light piercing sultry air,
a mere worm but a luminous spotlight
of nothing more than desire.

2.

Fireflies in Liguria in May.
They appear to climb the stairs –
one, two, three, four, five –
and then drift around the terrace
with luminous intent. Now,
one trips into view, a quizzical newcomer,
simply seeking out another of its kind.

3.

One night when the electricity failed,
we lit candles, filled our glasses
and headed to the window.
What lights! Beneath us in the olive grove
a stream of fireflies flew to and fro,

a phosphorescent flash mob, their delicate light
optimism's brightest retort to darkness.

4.

Mid-Atlantic, five hundred miles off Mauritania.
The moon's crescent just disappeared.
The darkness is total, sky and sea merged,
stars lost in water. Then we see them,
explosions, no other word will do,
detonating the ocean, shatters of beauty,
split seconds of aqueous light
and then only darkness until
the very next explosion.

Notes from the Ocean

Dolphins nudge
each other
at the bow
and then a push
of momentum
and they're out,
accelerating
into the ocean,
slamming on the brakes
and turning back
to do it again
and again.

~

A prison of ocean
encloses us all.
There is no escape.
A prison of fear
ensnares my thoughts.
The light of experience
suggests a way forward.
I wander as if in a dream.
A prism of a rainbow

glides across the ocean
towards me and only me.

~

I sing what I cannot understand.
I mouth the words because I know too much.
Volume is not meaning;
silence is not understanding.
I am standing at the stern,
my arms aloft, looking back,
bidding farewell to what have I missed,
and what I failed to make sense of.

~

Ten days without washing,
we stand on deck embracing a rain shower.
The rain is cold. It stings our sunburnt backs.
Then we warm. We put soap on our bodies
and the real downpour arrives.
Rain and rain and rain. Off the sails
it flows, then gushes. It slides
over our sun creamed skin,
so we can feel pores coming alive.
Water renews.

~

Slight is the thing which bends.
It is a filigree twisted into strength.
Flight is the thing which ends
with the withering wind and
begins our motion through the seas.

~

Songs make sense of the night.
On watch at four a.m. we retrieve
a night in a bar in Dublin
and the words of the *Wild Rover*.
I see Danny the Ducie fiddler
with his beatific expression
going through his Friday paces
and George the toothless barman
who played the spoons and downed Guinness
with the restless stealth of the guilty.

~

Spotted East of Guadalupe:
a red-billed tropical bird.
Then we knew we'd arrived.
The bird circled the boat not once but twice,
curious at this strange sighting,
a wandering dream in rough watery reality,
a tropical figment in a world of sunlit glimpses.
It appeared to pause and then headed away,
its long tail bearing off with the wind.

~

If it was easy everyone would do it.
Discomfort and the imprisonment of days
are the true coinage of experience.
Over the time staring to sea
we are building our own currency
which will lie in our minds
as a hard-won and deserved treasure.
It can be shared but never repeated.

~

I have never understood that urge to tweak,
to change and alter in the name of improvement.
Why tinker when the weather is set fair
and we are on course? Sailing is an art.
There is science, but all sailors
believe they are artisans of the breeze,
tailoring their sails to an exact angle
every time, reeling in and letting out
the genoa when the timing is spot on.
Art is improvement –
the final brushstroke, the change of tint,
the vital word added to proofs,
the touch of the chisel on the capstone.
Science is explanation
and, in time, even the wind on the sails
and the waves on our bow will be explained.

~

After sixty metres the depth gauge goes blank,
too much sea to contemplate.
Sometimes at night the gauge flashes –
often mysteriously at 78 metres.
I imagine a whale swimming beneath us,
bemused at the blank black space above,
keeping us company for a mile or two
and then diving deeper and deeper.

~

The fish fight. Twenty minutes
and then the line snaps dead.
We had readied the grill and the limes
so sit and wait for another

to take the hook, diving long and deep,
wriggling for life on the surface
before being landed, killed
and prepared within the hour.
The fish tastes of life, vigour undimmed,
purity of spirit and diet,
and cooked up on a plate for us.

~

As I sleep the Atlantic is alive.
I can hear the swoosh and inhalations
of water like wet urgent breaths
somewhere through the hull.
The sea rushes back and then,
with a giant exhalation, pushes
us forward. Push and shove,
glide and grate, the sea is force,
power at our sides, coaxing
life where none existed, renewing
with each fresh wash of sound.

~

A prayer is extinguished by the salty wind
and what sounds like a cry
is heard and fades at our beam.
What voices of the seas are these?
Onwards we sail. The air is sugared and tropical,
Barbados threatens to come into view
but then disappoints us, hidden from our eyes.
The seas are never silent. The winds
winnow through the waves, sibilant
with movement, a fizz of Atlantic life

comes in glad response. What swirls
of current, circles teased from the straight,
the force of waves captured in an angle.
For the Atlantic, the land is the myth.
This is the ultimate force, watery cradle of being.

Reefing at Three a.m.

After a day of lazy progress,
she took off at six and flew,
from five to eight knots, the sea
suddenly alive, the wind pushing
and pushing and pushing. Then rain,
a squall became a torrent.
Three figures stand in cabin darkness
clothed head to toe in waterproofs,
faceless, trawler-industrial.
With their head lamps on they come alive
and climb the wooden steps to the rain.
I lie in my cot and can see their red lights
as they go about taking the mainsail down a reef.
In the dark moonlight it is mechanical.
Only calls and commands add humanity.
After ten minutes or so they return
and remove their waterproofs slowly and damply.
One who didn't have time to change is soaked
to the body, a tropical chill settling on him.
They compare notes on the rain and the wind
and then slip back to their beds.
The boat moves on, flapping,
knocking, shaking, into the fierce night.

Men on a Boat

There is no meaning,
only the journey to meaning.
There is no end,
only the reaching towards an end.

What do they want from the journey?
Not to escape, they say;
not to reinvent themselves;
not to discover meaning;
not for love nor friendship.
They are here for the trip,
the *craic*, the feeling of simply
doing something, the accomplishment,
for completion; A to B, that's it,
enough and no more.

There is no purpose,
only the need for some completion.
There is no destiny,
only the warm flow of the current.
There is no reward,
only the sense of otherness.
There is no wind,

only a long, lingering swell
lifting us upwards and then down.
There is no hope,
only their hands on the wheel.
There is no one else,
only you and the sea and the world.

The Passenger

The only passenger on the ship,
I know nothing of knots and reefs.
And so, I head to the galley
and the swinging hob and oven.
I chop and peel, fry and boil.
This desire to be useful
is deeply engrained. I want to please
yet it feels a hollow gesture.
While others pull at ropes,
I empty the fridge, tidy a lettuce
and gaze out of the narrow port hole.
I am at sea, my role unclear,
ambiguity rules.
In the afternoon I have my watch.
Staring out to sea is the best work I do.

Sea Letters

An email from mid-Atlantic.
Potatoes are boiling in the galley
and Sufjan Stevens is playing.
Five kilometers of water beneath us,
surrounded by the horizon
and I am typing your name
and my heart is beating with yours.

~

You can never know the moment.
Not truly. But, it is there suddenly,
a feeling of moving beyond what was
to what can be, no, what will be.
It is destined. You are powerless,
yet omnipotent. It is vital.
You are short of breath, gasping uncertainty.
The moment is here and your life has changed.

~

The hours of a dozen Atlantic nights have passed.
The gibbous moon shines. Stars fill the sky
to unimagined dimensions.
Sails move in the wind.

And so we are apart.
I feel only stillness and our completeness.

~

Some things you have chosen.
Others have happened – often wonderfully –
but the power of choice wields
a different sway over your feelings.
I have chosen you, you have chosen me.
"You come into the world alone
and leave it the same way,"
a shaven-headed guru told me
as we stood viewing the frozen Baltic.
I shivered, not from the cold,
but from the lonely thought.
There is no denying the truth of it.
The world is gloriously peopled
and wonderfully empty of emotion.
We are here then gone,
like the rainbows in our wake.

~

You never knew beauty until that day.
In the past it had been an imperfect measure.
Then it was there in front of you:
That was what was meant by beauty,
that was what all the fuss was about.
A silent gasp was your only expression.
This was beauty and all you needed to know
was where it would lead you.

~

There is a tulip in the ocean,
floating beside us, cresting a wave
and then keening on. The tulip
is purple, its bud still tight.
Its green stem reflects the light
and shines in the dark Atlantic.
There is a tulip in the ocean
as if you were beside me always.

Our Rainbow

We are running at six rainbows a day.
Sometimes it is just the luminous root
of a rainbow on the horizon.
Sometimes it is the full-blown glorious arch
stretching miles to the clouds.

Yesterday, a rainbow chased us.
It emerged from the sea and its ends
seemed to hover horizontally
until they almost touched us,
a rainbow magnet pulling us towards it.

We haven't sighted a ship for three days.
There is no one near us.
Just five thousand metres of water,
a cloudy sky, and the latest rainbow,
our rainbow, possessed and destined to fade.

The Smell of Land

Twelve days without a glimpse of land,
three days without a ship in sight,
even the dolphins are absent.
All we have are the petrels and shearwaters,
flying fish and the rolling ocean.
We sit endlessly on deck and watch.
It is an every-changing tableau
of blues, blacks and aquas. You look
and think you have a glimpse of something,
an animal, a great fish, a piece of debris,
but, no, nothing again, simply the ocean
and the sky which becomes part of the ocean
and the air warm and heavy. Soon it will change.
Gulls and cormorants will appear,
the sea will shallow and land will slowly rise,
a light in a house, a twinkling port.
It is said that you can smell land from miles out.
It is there before you can see it,
rotting, poisoned, heated like garden compost,
steam rising and lights dimming the sky.

North Atlantic Moonlight

Mystifyingly bright,
the moon lights the sky,
yellow as never before,
luminescent.
The sky divides –
two thirds starlight,
one third moonlight.
No clouds, the dark sea
pulsing and little more,
the wind tensing the sails
and then releasing, tensing
then releasing. On watch,
we dutifully scan the horizon
mistaking stars for boat lights.
Slowly the moon slips down,
clouds flit in and out,
brightness fades as we watch,
a perfect departure, and still
a final glimmer of yellowness
until the darkness is total
and the stars regain brilliance,
shooting stars thrown asunder,
so quick, you miss them,

so bright, your breath skips
a moment in excitement.

What we are seeing is the extinguishing of light;
what we are feeling is the amazement of night;
what we are breathing is black starlit fulfilment.

Water Maker

A bucket in the sea.
I stand at the boat's edge,
my legs pressed against the guard rails,
an old rope in my hands
attached to a black bucket.
I pick a wave and dip the bucket in.
It is taken with the water and dragged.
It is a battle to lift it now.
I struggle, my arm tensing with effort,
and the bucket skitters along the top water.
Eventually, it lifts above the water
and I pull in with the old rope
up into the boat above the rail.
The water is clean warm,
I look into it expecting life of some sort
– a fish perhaps, a shell, a trail of seaweed –
but see only purity and light.

Night Watch

1.

Three hours on night watch
lazily scanning the night,
watching the boat's image
travel across a screen,
tweaking the steering
from time to time.
Three a.m. to six a.m.
disappears like night.
I hand over and log the details
– a few more miles done,
our speed over ground,
wind speed and tap the barometer.
I climb into bed and feel my back.
The sheets and pillow are sea damp,
like my clothes and my browning skin.
I am moved from side to side by the boat's rolling.
Sometimes it seems to come to a halt.
Then there is silence except for water
streaming by, a few inches away.
Soon I fall asleep. My watch is done.

2.

All is darkness.
Darkness as we have never known.
The moon is behind us,
tucked behind a cloud.
Stars complete the world.
I trace a satellite,
a weak light tracking night,
and sketch shapes between stars.
I believe I can see a ship
but it is a star which has fallen
to the cusp of blackness
which is the end of the world.

Log Book

There is order here.
Numbers in rows every three hours,
the story of a watch.
Speed over ground. Wind speed.
Nautical miles covered.
Longitude. Latitude.
All is neat and tidy.
Outside the wind is rising
– 30 knots – rain is coming
and we are sipping soup
looking to the filling sky.

A Squall

Four a.m. east of Martinique,
the clouds are cartoon cathedrals
behind us and around us.
Through the darkness we can sense the rain,
running towards us in the night.
When it comes it begins gently
and then works up to a downpour.
The wind moves to thirty knots
and the moon and the stars disappear.
We sit in the cockpit. The boat handles well,
downwind and balanced,
accelerating and then slowing
with the swell and the winds.
Now, the clouds are directly above us –
dark masses of vapour and rain –
sitting there seeming unwilling to ever move.
But they do. The winds ease
and the clouds move on.
The moon comes out again,
the stars illuminate us once more,
and we breathe easily until the next
Atlantic squall comes along.

Passing Barbados

Tony Cozier from Bridgetown,
Port of Spain, and elsewhere.
Late at night and the cricket is a whisper
on a short-wave radio. Roberts and Holding,
Garner and Marshall, Walsh and Ambrose,
athletes, sprinters, lopers,
the ball fizzing off hard-baked ground
and the batsmen hopping, hoping,
twitching, jabbing. The rich, long
vowels of the commentary, like islands.
Michael Holding off his long run,
a four hundred metre runner,
swapping the ball from left to right hand
half way through his long glide in.
And then the point of delivery,
smooth yet dynamic, the ball leaving his hand
an unfathomable missile. The batsman hardly
moves as the ball slams into him. A reprieve.
Under the bed sheets I can feel the relief,
a stay of execution. I go to sleep as Cozier purrs
and resolve to rise early to check the score.

A Buoy's Story

The mid-Atlantic buoy.
What must it see? Who does it warn?
Hundreds of miles from land
it charts the rise and fall of the waves,
precipitation, wind speed, ocean rain.
What would John McLean have made of it?
He went up and down the Clyde on *The Torch*
inspecting and fixing buoys on muddy banks
and in swirling brown waters.
A step from the ship and he was on,
opening the access hatch,
fiddling with the wires and bulbs.
He never learned to swim,
preferring to take his chances.
Armed with a dram and a lager
he would say that it was just a job,
the same as mending washing machines
and all the other things he brought back
from the mechanical dead.
I can see him now – cardigan,
neat moustache, heading out
to find a screwdriver,
leaving his drinks unattended.

I never remember him actually drinking.
Instead, alcohol was absorbed as he passed
from one job to another, the immaculate workman,
happy to do, to fix, to solve;
from such small acts comes greatness of purpose.

Looking to Sea

Rejoice at the unknown, celebrate the darkness.
How long can you look at the sea?
Endless days is the answer.
How long can you look at the night sky?
Endless nights and more.
Beyond the sky and the sea
there is nothing. And so, we look
for hour upon hour for a chink of meaning,
an other world glimmer of explanation.
It doesn't come but the more we look
the more we tease greater depth
from the blackness above and below.
Beyond the stars there are further constellations
and deep under the sea undiscovered citadels.

Morning Sun

Caribbean sun at eight a.m.
It has no need to warm up,
but arrives at full glorious heat.
It stings my back as I look to sea.
No seasons, just wet and dry here;
none of the subtle juxtapositions
of emergence and decay, but pure heat.

As a child he would go out running
with his father at 5.15 a.m.
Light would come through within the half hour.
Now, his father is beyond running
but can maintain a brisk medium pace,
remembering the stretch of muscles,
the pride of being there with his son,
their steps in unison and the heat
primed to emerge fully formed.

Dominoes at Sea

Civilising places we built churches,
bureaucracies and prisons;
brought our games as recreational jewellery.
Golf on the moon, dominoes at sea.
Our game is illuminated by a head torch.
This is the theatre of dreams,
four men crouched around a table,
dominoes clacking as they hit wood.
Close your eyes and it is some Greek *kafenion*.
Around us, the swell rolls,
waves collide with the beam,
sails flap from time to time.
But the world is no more. This is it:
a light, a game, time slipping.

Slow Weather

Here the weather comes slowly.
It is hatched in the distance
and then stretches towards us,
like a body awakening from sleep,
a friendly flexing, clouds nudging
against blueness, a gentle shoulder charge.
In time, hours not minutes, darkness
sits above us, the humid air
tightens noose-like and the rain begins.

End Signs

On the back of the boat, your father's flag,
a souvenir of VE Day, in a drawer for years
and now frayed but fluttering as we come into
St George's, Grenada. Imagine his surprise
if he'd seen us, his son and his boat,
moving through the clear Caribbean Sea,
heading into port, our first taste of Carib
and a chicken roti at the Nutmeg café.
It would have been unimaginable.
What is now fact was once impossible;
what was beyond us, now achievable.
And now the flag is put away,
a story for tomorrow's impossibles.

PART 2: LAND

Land is apart

Salita Priaro

It begins in the water. The slipway.
Napoleon's ships eased from here
into the Ligurian Sea.
Now, I stand with my trousers rolled,
my feet in the water, the dull crawl
of the sludge between my toes
and the smell of sea, oil and fried fish in the air.
The aperitivo drinkers stare. My feet
are x-ray white in the cold water, my bones
atop the rotting shore debris, nylon net slivers,
the miniscule bones of hundreds of unloaded fish.

Life begins.

From the slipway I can see the gradual slope.
In the wall there is a shrine.
The blessed Lady protects.
I begin walking. Slowly and slowly still.
Walking. My feet and calves
drop seawater onto the hot concrete.
The drinkers return to their campari sodas
and I move up the hill towards the first steps.

Focaccia, fresh fish, funerals. No bright lights,
just the tikka tikka of daily conversation.
I bow and let my hand sweep the step ahead.
It is warm to the touch, sand fills the gaps.
Looking up, I see light. Tikka tikka.
A washing machine shifts cycles in an apartment,
a canary sings and I come to rest on a step.

A few more steps and then the corner shop.
"Ciao!" says the owner as he unloads a box.
Inside, I know, there is a line of shoppers
and a tattooed woman behind the counter.

I drink water.
Now, the steps are more uniform. I count them.
One, two, three, four, five, six, seven ...
There is a lemon in the middle of the steps.
It is resting against the angle of stone, ant covered.
I am climbing to the sun, a lemon in my pocket.

A family is sitting outside beside the steps.
There is a bottle of wine on the table, prosciutto.
They are framed in the arthritic hold
of an old wisteria, gingerly supported.
Its blossoms delicately litter the steps ahead.

One Hundred

Our children will live one hundred years or more.
Our grandchildren will likely live one hundred and ten.
Pity them, the tired stretching decades,
the false starts and dashed hopes, dreams undone,
and then undone again, ticked wish lists.

~

Imagine Takayama in Gifu prefecture.
The snows have gone. Wooden shutters are closed.
Charcoal burns somewhere, a dog is barking.
A car slides down a nearby street.
I push on a door and it opens. There is one man.
I push on another door. There is no one.

~

Empty years build into lives. I take your hand.
Together. The seasons are time's tourniquet,
tightening and stretching, bonsai twists
in a dream world of straight pines and high sun.

~

In the bar by the sea there is a diving suit,
a brass-buckled bowl of a helmet
and thick fabric, a marquee of trousers,

and leaden clown boots. A tube of air.
Outside is out-of-season, even the sea,
December brown not June's blue.
Down the main street there is a flood channel.
Melted snow fills this deep concrete trough
for five days a year, purely flowing to its salty end.

~

I am one hundred years old.
The world is emptying like snow from the mountains.
The shutters are closed and yet light comes through.
I sit on my chair with a book I never read.
Someone is practising the saxophone and,
as they reach an amateur crescendo,
the church bells ring. I count the chimes.
Make a wish! A scooter passes on the road
and a train tunnels beneath the olive grove.
I can hear my heart beating.

Still.

Autumn Morning

For Barnaby

A deep shroud covers the beech hill.
The dog disappears into the dewy undergrowth
and my mind is thousands of miles away
in an air-con cool hospital room.

Only 23 weeks, he couldn't have lived.
All that will remain of him is an unsaid name.
It lingers in the damp air as I whisper it,
trying out what will never be shouted,
a mummer's murmur of being.

But that is not all. A momentary life
and yet there is more than a mere whisper
left behind for us to hold, much more.

What remains with us is the slow fading pain.
What remains with us is an imagined future,
a life of what-might-have-beens, hopes held
and cherished in the face of what's real.

What remains is love. We know this
and we know it as an immutable fact.

His life was hardly lived but we know love.
On an Autumn morning we know love
and that is almost enough to dry tears.

All That Is Remembered

All that is remembered sleeps with me now.
It is there. The baggage of being.
I close my eyes, yet can feel its weight.
Where I have been, who I am, what I have felt.

All that I have forgotten exists,
some personal half-life, echoing my being
and yet out of reach, endlessly;
where I have been, who I am, what I have felt.

All that I am is here at this moment with you.
Where we are going and what we are doing
matters little. We go. We are. We do.
Where I am, who I am, what I feel.
Where you are, who you are, what you feel.

Sense of Confidence

The momentum of life stills.
Suddenly work in the morning pales,
a dull sinking feeling and then
the ennui of departure. A day,
like hundreds, thousands, of others,
and energy slipping away.
Mid-morning you lean back, yawn
and sigh, as if the fight has gone.
You can no longer wrestle with chance,
no longer chase the next job.
Instead, you sit down with a green tea
and rest silently. Doing nothing is a skill
you haven't needed for years. But now,
one thing after another has gone.
You make a list of what needs to be done,
sigh again. It is confidence,
a feeling of getting somewhere,
moving forward, a plan of sorts.
It has gone and may never return.
So, what now if certainty is no more?
The anxious fudging of days into months,
the disappointment of days ill spent
and the shade of failure falling.

The Beginning of Love

In the beginning of love the chiffonnière began gathering the
    granular patina of age. The clock in the corridor echoed chimes
    and the smell of soup slipped into our nostrils.

In the beginning of love the horse stood on the hill and the sun
    shone on its flanks. The woods were beech-stilled and cooled
    and a buzzard stood idly on a branch above us.

In the beginning of love I took a turning on a May evening,
    parked outside your house, and the car dripped oil onto the
    road and ticked itself cool as we opened red wine.

In the beginning of love time stretched long and taut; endlessly
    now. In Arezzo, the café, cappuccino and brioche, the wait
    until it was decent to order wine.

In the beginning of love the sun shone through trees and milk-
    coloured clouds bridged to blue sky. Two christened birds
    returned day after day to the same wire.

In the beginning of love we felt we knew the world;
    understanding spread inside us, a welcome side effect of desire
    and, with understanding, light.

In the beginning of love your breath fell on the back of my neck
and I could feel my heart beating faster and faster so that every
beat coined a new day.

In the beginning of love a bicycle race outside Livorno, the
road filled with cyclists, stretching in readiness and, us, quiet
bystanders, the day's heat rising.

Confessional

I am my own confessional.
Not the chagrin of Stolichnaya folly,
not bed and breakfast liaisons,
nor behind hands whispers of troubles,
but the dulling beat of failure,
the tremulous fanfare of mundanity.
What might have been has gone.
What I could be is here and now.

Fingering the stem of my glass,
I confess it all. I have failed
the dream of myself, the impostor;
I am an empty page, a lattice grill
and inside a dusty box and bench;
hard dark wood and a stone floor.

A surplice is on a hook. The organ plays.
I drop a euro into the box. It echoes
with my steps as I make an escape,
the latest in a life of near misses,
to the café de la cathédrale
where I find a priest with a café noir,
La Croix, and his friend's pet poodle.

Childish Thoughts

1.

Child in my eyes still,
even now she is a woman,
illuminated by sunlight,
raising an eyebrow as a question,
and knowing that was all that was needed.

2.

Crucibles are what make us,
events which slip from our grasp,
islands of painful education,
revealing us as we truly are:
Artfully strong in the burning heat.

3.

Capturing the moment wasn't hard.
Every tissue and atom talked of love.
In your arms our newborn child
raising a finger as she sucked,
able to convey love at an instant.

4.

Confidence is hard-won and yet
every time in a strange situation,
in an unknown group, you'd
rally a friendship from nothing,
a purposeful stride and then your name.

5.

Call the question: what is love?
Elusive is the answer, if any.
In your name it becomes clear,
rising from instinct and knowledge,
an implicit, unsaid, understanding.

6.

Calling people after the birth,
everyone asks for the weight and name.
Is that with a k? I before e?
Replying, I concentrate, this is all now,
a name is a new beginning.

7.

Character comes pre-set but
experience adds the ballast.
Inside, you have decided,
railing against what you are told,
and, in the face off, you win.

8.

Call it what you like. I say, red.
Experimentation turns it blonde,
indeterminate russet and more.
Red is what it is, beautiful,
arranged like skeins of silk.

9.

Curious, what you remember.
Events so negligible to be forgotten
install themselves in our minds.
Re-arranging the supermarket beans
and putting our car keys behind them.

10.

Casual insouciance disappears,
every unposed image is overtaken
in time by a considered smile,
raising an eyebrow, your hair moved
a fraction to one side; a woman.

11.

Catching the time when we were closest –
events crowd out so many –
in the aftermath of an accident,
racing down a slope together,
all of these distilled into a life's mélange.

12.

Caught in the camera, your expression
eludes instant understanding.
Is it questioning, irritated?
Recalling that day, I can see the corn
and the dog springing like a newborn.

13.

Children enter the world and then
evade its grasp for years
in creating their true selves.
Ready, they dive straight in
and emerge spluttering to go again.

Days

The first day I couldn't remember everything that had happened
in my life was clear and cloudless. Somehow I could feel it.
The spaghetti jumble of memory unravelled and the ends were
severed; simply straightened.

The day the postman cycled through the yard clutching a
telegram was the last day of life. I knew the news it contained.
I knew it. My only child dead at sea. My only child! How
could that be? How could that be just?

I took the telegram, folded it and placed it in the pocket at the
front of my red apron. I said, thank you, of course. 'Aren't you
going to open it?' asked Harold. 'No. Never,' I said and walked
past the water trough to the kitchen door and inside.

Years later, my husband dropped down dead in the yard. It came
from nowhere. The boy was home by then but he was dead in
my mind and so, too, was I. The goose lay beside his body and
wouldn't let any one close until it grew too tired and hungry to
continue.

A day is always like any other. The sound of wagons going
through the ford, wind drifting through the willows, my hand

sliding over the window pane and smearing the dust into glass. Another day will be along. The day is long.

Night-time I sit on my chair by the window. I can see the turreted chimneys in the distance. That was once home, my fire smoking up and into the sky, my family spread across the farm and the land, sole figures illuminated by bright sun, cutting hay, playing with the cat. That day was once mine.

Running Out of Things to Say

I am running out of things to say.
I search in my mind and find nothing.
Why, I don't know. I have lived fifty or so years,
seen something of the world,
worked, loved, learned, enjoyed,
and desired many things.
But still the words won't come.
Perhaps I really do have nothing to say,
should accept it and move on to monkish silence.
What a disappointment that would be,
cast out to the conversational fringes,
silently standing there, awkward
from top to toe, disengaged,
and yet still feeling that the words will come.
I am running out of things to say.

Homing

Once or twice, perhaps more, I was given a lift to school by a
    family around the corner. No idea why.

I remember their house – cluttered, piles of shoes, clothes drying
    on radiators, toys, sporting accessories, a sofa buried in
    newspapers, art crowding the walls.

It felt like home but not like my home.

Later, there was a student house – lots of herbs, home cooking,
    books, music, decorative argument – which had the same
    effect: it felt like a home should be.

There was nothing wrong with my home. It was neat and tidy,
    everything away. It was filled with love, yes, but suffused with
    order and the regularity of things.

I can hear a clock ticking, the one in the kitchen,
and the heaviness of the curtains.

You think of home when you are far away,
when the rolling swell gathers behind you
and lifts the boat high above the ocean.

You think of home, the home of the imagination,
what it means rather than what it is,
warmth and love, life contained but freed.

Absence

Absence is the dullest of dull aches.
It questions and irritates, consumes itself.
And then, when you think it is complete,
it begins again. There is nothing positive,
a wrong turning, a road unfollowed.

The heart grows fond as you imagine love.
It can be in the next room, the next town;
absent a moment or almost a lifetime.
The heart grows fonder as surely
as my heart beat quickens
when I see you across the room.

The heart grows fonder even now,
years after we first met and still
it grows as you hold me in bed
and we lie there still as statues;
the beating antidote to absence.

With You

In bed: warmth and love.
The gurgle of heating and
our breath hanging in the cold air.
Our breath in the air.
Warmth and love.

A hot-bodied morning stretch,
my body against yours.
Our breath hangs in the cold air
and we can hear the cars in the rain,
their tyres pushing the water aside.
In the darkness, I remember our feet
walking on Corsican sand, the sea
deep of deepest blue, up to our knees
for mile after azure mile. Settled,
in the curve of your long back,
I feel sleep's dark contented pull.
Is this warmth love?
Is this love warmth?
I can hear your breathing;
the gradual rhythmic rise and fall,
the constancy of desire, being, in love.

Last Orders

This ocean is not your terrain.
You preferred concrete and tarmac,
city centres never suburbs,
bars rather than pubs.
Venturing abroad you drank yourself home.
In Spain, with your two-timing dad,
it was the brandy, a bottle a day,
and then the *cañas* to soothe the silence.
In Greece I recall a beach and you,
dressed for it, but at home in a beach bar.
Christ knows how much ouzo we did that week.
Drink was the death of you.
We should have known.
Double orders before the bell rang,
the constant enthusiasm for more and more.
We should have known but thought nothing of it.
You died in Tottenham, in a bath,
not extolling Lorca and *duende* in Andalucía
nor swapping stories with Seamus in Mossbawn.
A sad seedy death – you'd have appreciated that –
for a mandolin-playing lover of beauty
in a tuneless ugly world. You'd have loved
the funeral: the Northern Cemetery, wintry dark,

friendly, random human detritus gathered,
life's additions for a believer in subtractions.

Flying to Tokyo

O what can you say
when you have thought and done so little?
The lights are floating in the sea.
I count hundreds.
I think of swimming in the black water,
coming up for air, and then, the gasp,
and the light of a thousand fountains of light.

O what can you say?
The lights are dimmed as we linger over Siberia.
I drink a final rioja with Bob Dylan
in the endless imagined highlands.
It is dark but dawn in Tokyo. London time
hangs over us, like the habit of dullness,
clinging to the air, and now, the grasp
and the fright of a hundred disappointments.

O the experience.
Three weeks in Italy. Nothing to report,
apart from market days, the reddening grapes,
and the tautness of our calves from the stairs.
The ordinary is the experience.
I draw a blank, whiteness, the ring of a glass,

coiling and spreading on the table cloth,
and the taste, vital, red, like blood.

Deep Water

It must have been 1976,
somewhere off Hyannis,
jumping from the back of a yacht
into the summer-cool Atlantic.
Still, in my mind now,
I am falling through the water,
purblind blackness and depth
I had never encountered before
or even contemplated. Water
and still more water, down and down.
The sea had always previously been grounded,
the squish of Irish Sea sand between my toes,
brown swirling water, the stink of donkeys,
and the face-burning English sun.

Down and down until I reached an end point,
not my own but the choice of the ocean.
At the end point I feel silence. I feel it.
And then a rush of panic.
How could I fall so far?
Then the desperate climb to distant blinking light.

I break water.

Thirty years on in China the heat is blistering.
The Russian downstairs opens beer bottles
with his teeth and hands them to me.
The resort was once for party members.
Now, Russians gorge themselves,
big ugly men and elaborately decorated women,
ordering course after course, a pyramid of plates.
At the beach the sand burns. The sea
is clammy, warm and salty, a hazy soup.
One hundred metres out from shore
I feel my hand touch something, then another,
a shoal of jellyfish. I swim frantically,
cramp freezes my right leg, and am breathless
when my feet touch the fiery sand again.

Breathing

Deep breaths of words.
I am speaking to the sky.
What do I know?
I know nothing.
What do I see?
I see the world
and the rocky promontory.
What do I feel?
I feel nothing.
Yet seeing is feeling
and I see the road,
the cars curving up the hill,
the trains streaming into the tunnel,
the boat coming into port.
I see it all and feel nothing.
I am a peripheral spirit,
a name tagged on,
a figment of friendship,
poised like a decorative leaf
and then dropped, falling to ground.

Old Friends

Friends lost. The list lengthens.
Whether through discord or ennui,
they fall away leaving a handful
of names and faces, friends chanced upon,
friendships forged in unlikely places
and still there after years.
What becomes of friends lost?
They linger guiltily in our minds,
mildly toxic, tarnished by thoughts
of what really happened, what was said,
what passed one by as our paths parted.

Headline, No Story

I am the headline writer,
the glib snatcher of words,
pun player, fact stretcher.
What does that say about me?
A desire to condense perhaps,
to make words count,
to get to the nub of it all,
and then to leave it at that.
Forget the story, enjoy the headline,
that's the thing: I am a splash
of words with no story, all front,
lacking depth. Or, I am a distiller
of truth, a pithy layer-out of hard facts,
the truest voice in a world of doubters.
I knew once I was the headline
and the story. Now, the story eludes me.

Autograph Collection

1. Seamus Heaney

His name is on the piece of paper. He signed it.
The signature is a condensed lope of letters,
rounded, flowing from christian to surname.
What does it prove? Nothing in itself,
but it is my proof that I was there in the room,
a cold Wednesday night in a draughty hall,
his voice alive, rhyming to the ceiling.
In the papers a few days later,
I learn it was the night his mother died.
And there he was, in front of me,
his fountain pen worn by years of use,
blowing on the ink of his name to make it dry.

2. George Best

George and Matt Busby, a policeman,
black and white, the European Cup,
enormous in George's hands,
and the smiles big as Wembley.
A dream made real right there,
a different world of feints,
effortless over the ground,
light footed quickness, in his element,

the right time. Years later, ruined by drink,
he signed his name on a light patch,
part of a tired promo deal to sell shirts.
He signed hundreds in a day
and I have one framed on the landing.
Every night going to bed I see them,
George and Matt, gloriously happy,
for that moment, their feet on the grass,
the result a chime of numbers, 4-1,
the names on the trophy a rhyme of greats.

3. Johnny Giles

Greenock, Cappielow Park –
is it even called that now? –
pre-season, a good crowd in
for the champions of England,
warming up, leg stretching,
hard pros, uninterested.
In the tunnel after the game,
being pushed forward by Daniel,
his red face, collar, tie and V-neck,
hands pushing my back.
"Johnny, an autograph for the boy,
he's come all the way from England."
And the player looking up to Daniel,
a stranger talking as if he knows him,
must be used to it I suppose, and me
with a programme in my hand,
just a few scrappy pages and the teams,
and a pen which the player takes.
He scribbles his name and Daniel is on,
pushing past people to Bobby Collins,

barrel-chested *generalissimo*,
"Great wee man, great, got a moment?".
Collins gives a gruff hello and walks on.
Daniel leaves it at that. Hand on my shoulder,
he escorts me back through the crowd.

Truth

In the words I have written there is truth.

In the wood I have worked on there is truth,
the sap-filled circles of life are sawdust smooth.
I run my hands over the wood. My cigarette burns.

In the note there is truth. Held in the warm air,
the note is out of context, a gorgeous blast,
my address to the atmosphere,
a white stone on the grey stoned beach.

Acknowledgements

Thanks are most of all due to Steve Litson for inviting me to become part of his dream and for his huge generosity of spirit, sense of humour and reserves of patience. Thank you also to Bill, Bruce and Denis for their sustaining friendship on board *Wandering Dream*.

A grateful thank you to Richard Burton for his honest, constructive and modernist feedback – as well as the years of happy lunches.

Thank you also to Rebecca Clare of Infinite Ideas for her attention to detail.

The cover photographs are by Steve Litson.

The photograph of the author is by Kim Durdant-Hollamby.

About the author

Stuart Crainer is a writer. He is the author of a number of non-fiction books on the subject of business. This is his first collection of poems. He lives in Berkshire and was brought up in Lancashire.